Foreword

In 1986 the study 'Training in the management of development organizations and their activities in Africa' was published by Novib. Since then new ideas and initiatives have come up. Considering Novib's continuous involvment in strengthening the NGO Sector in Africa, we felt it appropriate to commission a new study on this important issue. It is our opinion that the INTRAC team has come up with a very interesting and challenging document. We trust that all our readers will agree with Novib that for the years ahead the policies formulated in this document will be a guide in the implementation of the many I.D. activities, which will take place in Africa.

Hans Pelgröm
Director Projects
NOVIB

INTRAC:
Supporting the development of NGOs internationally

A SUMMARY DESCRIPTION:

Set up in 1991 to provide specially designed Management Training & Research Services for European NGOs involved in Relief and Development in the South – dedicated to improving organisational effectiveness and programme performance of Northern NGOs and Southern partners where appropriate.

Our goal is to serve NGOs in i) the exploration of the management, policy and human resource issues affecting their own organisational development, and ii) the evolution of more effective programmes of institutional development and cooperation.

INTRAC offers the complementary services of
Training,
Consultancy
and Research

within three themes
1) NGO Management and Organisation;
2) Improving Development Projects and Programmes;
3) Media Management and Policy Advocacy.

The following Report was written as a result of collaboration between Novib and INTRAC. Please contact either organisation for further details of future workshops or research on this important issue, which has already raised considerable interest.

INTRAC
PO Box 563
Oxford OX2 6RZ
UK
telephone: 44 (0)865 201851
fax: 44 (0)865 201852

INTRAC
Strengthening NGOs in the 1990s

Designed & produced by
Davies Burman Associates 0865 250079

© INTRAC 1992

ISBN 1 897748 00 0

Printed in Great Britain July 1992
Reprinted March 1994
Reprinted January 1996

Novib
Amaliastraat 7
2514 JC Den Haag
Telephone: 31 (0)70 3 421 621
Postgiro 64 53 00

Novib's Annual Report and Summary of Projects can be ordered with a payment of 10 guilden. The Annual Financial Report can be ordered separately for the price of 5 guilden. Orders should be made to Novib/Guest at Your Table, Department of Public Information,
telephone 31 (0)70 3 421 777.

Institutional Development & NGOs in Africa:

Policy Perspectives for European Development Agencies

Alan Fowler

with

Piers Campbell & Brian Pratt

Contents

1
Introduction

Institutional development is recognised as an important element in projects and programmes dedicated to the sustainable alleviation of poverty, the promotion of gender equity and achieving social justice for marginalized populations. Commissioned by the Netherlands Organisation for International Development Cooperation (NOVIB), the following pages provide an overview of NGO institutional development in the context of sub-Saharan Africa (SSA). It's primary purpose is to assist European NGOs formulate policies and strategies towards the institutional development of the NGO community on the subcontinent.

Because no field studies have been undertaken this report is limited in scope; its content draws mainly on the experience of INTRAC consultants. For this reason the coverage of SSA is uneven and the rapid changes on the continent mean that some items will be out of date almost as they are written. This report is not, therefore, a directory of resources available for institutional development (ID) within SSA. It does, however, provide (a) a systematic review of the "state of the art" in institutional development for NGOs; (b) an analysis of the demand and supply of institutional development services in Africa; (c) an outline of strategic decisions required from European NGOs wishing to support NGO institutional development in Africa; and (d) a simple checklist for ID decision-making. The literature used is included as Appendix I.

Why is institutional development believed to be particularly vital for successful implementation of development programmes and projects and especially in Africa? To answer this question, we begin in section 2 with a short history of institutional development and section 3 outlines the factors that have contributed to the growth and problems of African NGOs as development organisations. Clarification of the confusion surrounding the use of the terms "institution" and "organisation" is dealt with in section 4. Section 5 provides an overview of institutional development in practice.

Because the NGO community in Africa is diverse the study identifies, in section 6, the institutional development needs of two distinct types of African NGO – intermediary or service organisations and local community or people's organisations.

Section 7 assesses trends in the capacity within sub-Saharan Africa for supporting NGO institutional development. We review what is there, what is emerging and what, if anything, can be said about its quality. There are a number of policy issues of importance to European NGOs in decision-making

4

related to future assistance for institutional development in Africa and for African NGOs. Section 8 sets out these issues as well as identifying gaps, preferred practices and areas of priority.

As African partners become stronger and more capable the mutual performance and division of roles between European and African NGOs will be more critically assessed. This is already happening in some partnerships. In other words, strengthening the institutional capabilities of African NGOs will have complementary organisational consequences for European NGOs themselves. Section 9 reflects briefly on this trend.

2
The Importance of Institutions in Development

2.1 A Brief History

Under the heading "institution-building", the immediate post-independence period in Africa saw much energy spent on either creating new or strengthening existing state institutions. This effort was based on the idea that government institutions would be *the agents to induce and maintain the social and economic changes required for the overall task of "nation-building"*. State bodies were the primary focus of institution building efforts, heavily supported by external funders. The unit of concern for institution builders was a functional part of government organisation – a ministry, a department, a parastatal body and so on. At this time little attention was paid to the impact of the broader environment on the functioning of an organisation or of development itself.

By and large, the process of institution-building concentrated on increasing the skills, knowledge and professional capacities of staff. A number of new educational establishments were created to serve the substantial public sector demand for trained manpower. The Pan African Institutes for Development (PAID) and the Eastern and Southern African Management Training Institute (ESAMI) stem from this era.

Increasingly, evaluations showed that the performance of government development projects and programmes was indeed critically dependent on the functioning of institutions, but not only those of the state. NGOs, such as community-based, grassroots people's organisations became recognised as significant contributors to project effectiveness. Evaluation findings also indicated that the focus on organisations as the unit of intervention was misplaced. Improving organisational performance had to take a wider set of factors into account: of the policies, for example, that regulated the relations between development actors, including the private sector. Today, emphasis is being given to the creation of an 'enabling environment' for development action by all sections of society, not just the state.

The eighties, therefore, saw a shift in both official terminology and methods, with "institutional development" becoming the key term and the "useful" role of non-governmental organisations as intermediaries and active participants gaining greater importance. Through its own experience, the NGO community has also appreciated the need for institutional strengthening as a key factor in partnerships and self-reliance.

2.2 Why Stress Institutional Development?

Initially, institutional development has been stressed because of its functional role in development. Put simply, specialists argued that projects and programmes require competent organisations to turn labour, land, capital, technology and so on into ongoing improvements in people's lives. Economists emphasised the need for investment in organisations to ensure a return on investments in other areas. Institutional development is one route to "human capital" formation. This justification for institutional development is still powerful.

In functional terms, strong organisations at all social levels are seen to be critical for: (a) the cost-effective transformation of inputs into outputs, (b) ongoing participation of stakeholders (read: politicians, leaders, managers, employees, beneficiaries, households, groups, etc.); (c) the mobilization and regulation of local resources; (d) the resolution and management of conflicts; (e) effective control in the division of benefits; (f) the monitoring, evaluation and validation of externally supported change; and (g) the translation of government policies into practice.

The late eighties have, however, seen an additional, political, argument being openly voiced in support of institutional development of NGOs, particularly grassroots or people's organisations in Africa. The dominant Western concept of socio-economic development based on liberalism and market forces maintains that NGOs must be supported because of their political role within civil society. It is envisaged that people must be empowered to take over some aspects of development from the overbearing, autocratic, inefficient and corrupt states that have commonly ruled in Africa. NGOs must also provide countervailing power to government expansionism; strengthen people's ability to hold public servants and politicians accountable for their (in)actions; and, foster democratic change by expanding social pluralism.

In sum, today institutional development of NGOs is emphasised because of the expectation that they will: (i) ensure better and sustainable performance of projects and programmes, and (ii) democratise development and society. Greater official aid for the institutional development of NGOs is meant to increase their ability to "deliver" in these two areas.

3
Institutional Development and African NGOs

3.1 A Simple NGO Typology

So far we have not made clear distinctions between types of African NGOs. Because their institutional development needs differ it is necessary to do so. Broadly speaking this study is concerned with three types of voluntary development organisations in Africa. These are:

i. Service or intermediary NGOs that are not set up, or controlled by the beneficiary groups. Commonly, these are legally registered organisations with paid staff, providing development services such as credit, information, technology transfer, health care, water supplies, improved natural resource protection and so on. Many African partners to European NGOs, including networks, would fall into this category, as would local branches of European NGOs.

ii. Community-based organisations (CBOs) created by people for their own benefit. The most elementary grassroots organisations are households, but household members also form groups which can be distinctive because of gender, for example the womens' organisations found in Africa; or because of age, such as circumcision groups. There are, in addition, community organisations made up of men and women of all ages to structure and regulate social life. They are often informal in nature and fulfil traditional functions, such as mutual savings, but can also be more formal, created to take on developmental roles, such as water committees. A key distinction within community-based organisations is whether they are traditional and informal or "modern" and formal in the sense that they are recognised by the state's development system.

iii. Membership NGOs provide services and employ staff but are owned by those who should benefit from the services that the organisation provides. Cooperatives would fit this definition, as would member-based organisations such as ORAP in Zimbabwe and SIX-S in West Africa. The institutional development needs of these NGOs differ. However, the needs of membership NGOs can often be equated with those of both the service and community-based organisations. Our further analysis will, therefore, concentrate on these two types.

3.2 The Critical Need for NGO Institutional Development in Sub-Saharan Africa?

There is an emerging consensus that, in comparison with other continents, insufficient and weak institutions are a critical bottleneck to sustainable and more equitable development in Africa. Why is this? Three historical factors are significant for NGOs and CBOs

3.2.1 Service or intermediary NGOs

The growth of African service NGOs has been strongly shaped by colonialism, post-colonial politics of development and the funding priorities and practices of Northern development agencies. Early in their penetration of Africa, colonial powers were accompanied by christian welfare organisations, providing an initial model for formal non-state service delivery allied to colonial interests. In response to colonial oppression, Africa established indigenous welfare organisations. These organisations "straddled" urban and rural areas, mediated between the indigenous peoples and the colonial government, provided services very much on an ethnic, self-help, voluntary basis and went on to act as the mobilizing embryo for many of Africa's political parties.

After the second world war, a new breed of secular, humanitarian and ideologically based European and North American NGOs came into being, OXFAM being one example. These offered a new model of an NGO that was not simply assisting the colonial power but had autonomy in its perspectives and actions. Simultaneously, the formation of national political parties in Africa tended to separate but not divorce indigenous welfare from their mobilization function. Subsequently, independence opened the gate for all sorts of foreign NGOs that provided models for non-profit service delivery that reflected Northern values and organisational structures.

In the era after independence, the united effort said to be needed for nation building left little space for indigenous NGOs to take on an independent position as development actors. They were unable to adopt roles that ran counter to government policies or definitions of development. The single political party argued that as it embraced and represented everyone all organisations were part of the nation-building effort and were, therefore, subservient to it. The very concept of NGO autonomy was antithetical to the national development ethos. An oppositional role was also excluded and this dimension of African NGOs is relatively recent, dating back some five to ten years. Finally, the belief that development was done by the state concentrated resources in government institutions, leaving NGOs to fend for themselves, usually by seeking foreign support. Such assistance, with its associated fashions, priorities and conditions has helped to shape African NGOs as mirrors of the North, and has encouraged African governments to see the sector as a substitute and additional source of much needed foreign exchange.

Today, external funding of African service NGOs has reached such a level that the size of the NGO community within most African countries bears little relationship to the national economic base. The divorce of African service NGOs from the local economic reality can leave them severed from, and suspended above, those they are set up to serve. In the words of Kingston Kajese, they are 'rootless' and have a dependency syndrome.

With a few notable exceptions such as SIX-S in West Africa and ORAP in Zimbabwe – which are membership organisations – African service NGOs tend to reflect the structure and culture of their Northern partners, are divorced from traditional social organisations and are uncoupled from the local resource base.

3.2.2 Community-based organisations (CBOs)

The community-based organisations involved in externally supported development on the continent are also a product of colonial history. For, in order to overcome ethnic differences exploited by colonial powers, many African governments systematically negated traditional social organisations. The official view was that traditional associations reinforced an unwanted ethnic awareness and, through their values and practices, acted as barriers to rapid growth and modernisation. In their place, governments imposed models of social cooperation at the local level that were to contribute to nation building. Socialist states tended to be more emphatic in this effort, with the party and cooperatives sometimes becoming almost the only vehicles allowed for people to organise themselves developmentally: an extreme example of this phenomenon is the peasant associations in Ethiopia.

The single party states that dominate Africa's political landscape became tightly woven with the control-oriented colonial bureaucracies they inherited. As a result, and assisted by donor aid, African governments have dominated local development, restricting the freedom and autonomy of community-based organisation. There was also limited government investment to make these local organisations stronger. First, because the government needed all its resources to build a more effective bureaucracy and, second, because strengthening community-based organisations could increase their ability to take development into their own hands. Such a change might reduce their subordination to state-led development. In sum, until the late seventies state-dictated development was effectively a continuation of the top-down style and practices typical of the colonial era. With limited resources set against great material demands NGOs could do little to make good the non-material institutional development needs of community organisations.

The past few years have shown the resilience of traditional community-based organisations, despite government attempts to deny or suppress them. There are increasing signs that traditional forms of social organisation, trusted by their members, are taking on a greater number of functions. For example, in Ethiopia during the power vacuum left by Mengistu, traditional leaders

10

became responsible in certain instances for local security, and were recognised and accepted as the legitimate decision-makers for the community. In addition, there is increasing evidence that more sustainable and equitable outcomes are likely to occur from externally initiated development projects if the CBO involved is one based on traditional structures rather than state imposition. This fact has significant consequences for European NGO donors that will be discussed later.

3.3 Institutional Development with African NGOs: a Serious and Difficult Challenge?

3.3.1 The effects of official aid

To the negative aspects of the preceding sections we can now add a rapid growth in expectations of what NGOs should and can do developmentally, combined with a more critical concern about their performance. The "rolling back of the state" through adjustment policies is swiftly allocating social roles and burdens to NGOs for which they are often ill prepared: hence the recent interest in NGO capabilities and absorptive capacity. Economic decline is also making NGOs more attractive as employers and as sources of political patronage, reinforcing their use for furthering self-interest rather than voluntarism.

The clearest example of the new official demand for stronger NGOs is given by the structural adjustment compensation programmes. In Ghana, Uganda and other African countries special programmes to mitigate the social costs of adjustment have been designed with a large NGO component. The overall design has taken place without substantial consultation with the NGO community which is left to negotiate on individual projects. One consequence of this trend is to provoke unhealthy competition and rivalry between local and foreign NGOs. As a result, NGO umbrella bodies have become fragmented and weak, making them less and less able to represent NGO interests effectively. Instances have been found where the UNDP Partners in Development Programme with NGOs has had the same effect. And the World Bank's efforts to mediate between governments and the NGO community using its finance as the carrot has not been positive in West Africa. Overall, the rapid growth in official aid for NGO work is stimulating the formation of a number of NGOs with little voluntary motive, nor skill in participatory action. Increasingly, African NGOs involve the existing political and bureaucratic elite in some way or the other.

This then raises the question: who is really being served by the new stress on institutional development – African people themselves or aid bureaucracies? In our view, the present emphasis on institutional development is developmentally correct. Increasing institutional differentiation is a fundamental characteristic of social advance based on capitalist economic relations and plural democracy. However, this being said, the way that institutional development is being defined and used serves donors more than recipients. This is not because aid agencies are inherently unjust but because they are not making (or are unable to make) the adaptations needed in order to reorganise themselves to work with NGOs. For example, UNDP believes that it can apply the same working methods to NGOs as it does to governments. The results of its efforts show that this is not the case and the NGO community has suffered in the process. Similarly, the World Bank has enormous difficulty in modifying its practices when dealing with NGOs, despite its stated commitment to do so. European NGOs also face similar problems (see section 9).

The point of significance is that, as things now stand, the official aid system is beginning to define the purpose of institutional development for NGOs to serve its own needs. This is happening, in part, because the NGO community has not (yet) got its act together with a mutually shared understanding of what ID is, who it is to serve and how it can be achieved as a distinct contribution within the aid system. By default, bi- and multilateral agencies are defining our future NGO community for us.

Overall, a situation has evolved where African service NGOs are expected to take on a substitutional role for the state. And, through new legislation, bureaucratic edict and greater volumes of official aid, NGOs are being more strongly drawn into the national system of a country's development administration as the lowest rung of the service delivery ladder. Yet this is not their only role in society. Service NGOs are seldom encouraged by governments to impact on policy formulation or to publicise the plight of the poor or the injustices they experience. Because NGOs – local and foreign – have their own perspectives and agendas, there is an ongoing uneasy relationship between them and African regimes.

It must, however, be born in mind in any discussion of African NGOs that they are a product of different forces and values from their European counterparts. European NGOs are founded on, and driven by, the imperatives of christian morality, justice, philanthropy and charity. African NGOs, however, tend to be expressions of colonial influence, funding criteria, self-interest and mutual self-help based on reciprocity as a dominant social value. Interpretations of differences in behaviour between African and European NGOs must take this into account.

3.3.2 Rapid environmental change
To the foregoing difficulties we need to add the issue of rapid change taking place in the political-economies and ecologies of many countries on the continent. Economically, virtually all states show a per capita decline in all important development indicators. But the burdens of decline are not being evenly distributed. The poor are becoming poorer, the poorest become impoverished and the already impoverished – particularly women and children – die. To the men made human problems of war and famine can be added the dynamics of

decreasing rainfall and drought that tax any administration. Africa's crises present NGO donors with a policy paradox. With the level of deprivation being what it is, virtually any assistance would reach those in need. But given the limited level of NGO finances shouldn't this dire situation call upon us to target our assistance even more sharply to those most in need? And, how do we balance the urgent short term responses of emergency relief and food aid with the long term strategies that sustained material and institutional development implies? One resolution of this dilemma is to recognise that whatever choices are made they have to be negotiated with, and carried by, local organisations. There is no viable alternative in the longer run. The question is, how to support local institutional development in a turbulent environment? This point is addressed later in the study (see sections 7 and 8).

Internal economic stress and global policy shifts that link aid to democratization are spurring internal political revolt – Zaire, Congo, Kenya. This instability gives both risks and opportunities for European NGOs. The risks are the waste of investment if a situation rapidly changes – for example, it is seen if someone is transferred, arrested or shot; or if the exchange rate becomes worthless and people steal to make ends meet; or again in a situation where riots and instability absorb people's time and energy, etc. However, windows of opportunity can open when a repressive regime is collapsing or adapting to the new reality. Progressive forces that emerge can be selectively assisted. Responding to this situation is another challenge faced by European NGOs.

3.3.3 The challenges: a summary

At the risk of gross generalization and with noted exceptions (that attract many funding agencies), given their history and circumstances it is no surprise that most African NGOs are constrained in their autonomy, are externally dependent, have ambiguous identity and are organisationally weak. Few satisfy the basic criteria of viability, autonomy of action, legitimacy and effectiveness by which an effective NGO should be measured.

Institutional development for NGOs in Africa is a serious challenge because we are dealing with a sector that: (a) is hardly institutionalised in terms of its (voluntary) values or identity; (b) is subject to increasing external pressures from official aid, (c) is expanding faster than is its ability to allow for the normal growth of internal cadres; (d) often lacks the ability to perform adequately; (e) has limited impact at the policy level; and (f) must operate in increasingly turbulent political environments and continuing economic decline.

The test for NGO institutional development in Africa is to redress this situation. The remainder of this study draws on those experiences to date that suggest how policies, practices and organisational change within European NGOs can assist African service NGOs and community-based organisations to take up this challenge.

4
What is Institutional Development?

4.1 Institutions and Organisations

Unclear and inconsistent terminology is one source of confusion in institutional development. Despite many attempts there is, so far, no water-tight definitional distinction to be made. There is, however, a reasonable consensus on the differences between an institution and an organisation. Present thinking and writing leads to the following definitions:

Institutions   Institutions are stable patterns of behaviour that are recognised and valued by society.

"Institutions, whether organisations or not, *are complexes of norms and behaviours that persist over time by serving collectively valued purposes.* Institutions can be concrete, like a nation's central bank or quite diffuse and general such as the institution of money." (Uphoff, 1986:9, emphasis in original)

Institutions exert themselves through rules, norms and values that influence people's lives. This obviously happens inside organisations but institutionalisation extends this to the wider social arena.

Organisations   Organisations are purposeful, structured, role-bound social units.

Put simply, organisations are collections of individuals who fulfil roles in order to realise common goals.

Organisations can become institutionalised as they acquire social value and stability.

For example, with its fifty years of history, its shops, its campaigns and public profile, OXFAM is an institution in Britain's voluntary landscape. Like NOVIB in Holland with its "Guest at Your Table" fund-raising and national campaigns, OXFAM is not just one of many developmental NGOs. Similarly, Save the Children Fund is institutionalised, but few others are – as yet.

Not all organisations are institutions and not all institutions are simply aggregations of organisations. Confusion in our understanding occurs because institutions and organisations overlap. First, because although differing in scope and permanency, both institutions and organisations shape and direct social behaviour. Second, day to day institutionalised social behaviour is largely expressed by the work of, and interactions between, people in organisations.

NGOs are engaging more and more in macro-policy reform: a level of action that is often institutional in its nature. However, most developmental work is principally concerned with organisations. *The emphasis of this study is therefore on institutional development that is organisationally based.* In other words, with organisational development that can have institutional outcomes.

To keep the distinction clear (although not watertight) throughout, we will use "institutional development" to refer to changes that are intended to occur outside any single organisation, in the patterns and arrangements of society: for example, it is applicable to changing the structure of relations between local level organisations and state agencies.

"Organisational development" will be restricted to activities that are aimed at change within an organisation, even if those changes are meant to help in its own institutionalisation.

Simply put, "institutional development" deals with changes that are meant to occur in social structures, "organisational development" with changes limited to organisations themselves.

5
Institutional and Organisational Development in Practice

What do the preceding sections mean practically for European NGOs? First, development-oriented agencies need to be aware of the distinction between change in social structures – the institutional dimension – as opposed to change at an organisational level. Second, because institutions transcend individual organisations, institutional development involves something broader than organisational development; this difference requires other goals, strategies, time scales and tools to bring about the desired changes.

5.1 Supporting Institutional Development

Support for the institutional development of NGOs in Africa tends to be strategic. An institutional development perspective will look at NGOs as a sector expressing values associated with voluntarism, self-help, self-reliance, countervailing power, social justice and so on; values that needs to be protected and extended. The rationale for financing institutional development will stem from the need to have a community of viable organisations and a change in the pattern of interactions between the NGO community and other development actors such as the state, official aid agencies and commercial enterprise. Institutional development will therefore aim at bringing change by:

1. *Building the foundations of the African NGO sector.* The issues here revolve around the number and diversity of non-governmental organisations – as service providers, as community groups, as people's movements, etc., – furthering the role they play in socio-economic development; ensuring greater accountability and responsibility; enhancing NGO ability to withstand external pressures, and so on.

2. *Enhancing collaboration and cooperation.* Supporting NGO networks, associations, Councils and other instruments to make NGOs a more cohesive force in national, regional and international development; stimulating and institutionalising NGO-based analysis of Africa's problems and articulation of NGO perspectives on how they can be tackled.

3. *Altering relations with the state.* Modifying NGO-state relations to give the sector greater autonomy of action; creating a more favourable policy

environment for NGO work; limiting potentially negative impacts of official aid; and gaining greater involvement of NGOs in national and local policy development.

The over-riding emphasis in supporting institutional development goes beyond simply improving the performance of individual NGOs *per se*, although this is important, but focuses on what they do collectively in and for society. We are, therefore, expecting to strengthen interactions within the NGO community as a way of reinforcing their position towards other institutional systems. The justification for resource allocations in institutional development relates to this overall view.

Many European NGOs have, or are formulating, strategic plans for regions and countries in Africa. Any such plan should address building the foundations of the sector, enhancing collaboration and altering NGOs' relations with the state. The approaches available for pursuing institutional development are varied. They include:

a. organisational development of strategically-oriented NGOs in Africa;
b. changes in the partnerships between European and African NGOs;
c. modification to funding practices of official aid agencies;
d. creation of new African NGOs, such as networks, that have multi-country institutional, rather than local, goals;
e. creation of national and international NGO support organisations to provide appropriate services to the NGO community;
f. creation and broadening of South-South NGO linkages and learning;
g. changing the relationship between service NGOs and community-based organisations;
h. helping increase NGO skills in policy analysis, negotiation and advocacy.

5.2 Organisational Development

5.2.1 Organisations as systems
Most of what people achieve in society is accomplished through organisations. And, organisations are a common instrument for changing institutions. A systems view can help us understand how organisations work and indicate what points of entry are available to change them. We can limit organisational systems to their formal boundaries (closed systems) or we can choose to include aspects of their external environment (open systems). By and large, developmental organisations, and especially NGOs, are very environmentally dependent. They are, therefore, most appropriately viewed as open systems because they cannot and should not be treated in isolation from the policies and organisational behaviour around them.

What does organisational development try to achieve? Lacking a universally accepted definition, we take organisational development to be an *ongoing process that optimizes an organisation's performance in relation to its goals, resources and environment(s).*

For historical and practical reasons organisational development has been equated with staff training. Experience shows that, while necessary, training is seldom effective in improving an organisation's functioning if it is not part of an overall OD programme.

As with other organisations, NGOs are built-up of a number of systems that need to be analyzed and changed. At least ten systems can be identified that provide points of entry for organisational development.

i.   A key system is the intervention or operational system, i.e. the way that an NGO actually does what it sets out do developmentally, including its gender recognition, technology choices, participatory methods, and so on. For an operational service NGO, like Save the Children Fund, ActionAid or PLAN, this is the system of change agents and types of activities through which the organisation directly engages with community-based organisations in their own institutional development. For donors, such as Bread for the World, OXFAM, NOVIB, etc., this is the primary process of prioritizing resource allocations, assessing proposals, disbursing funds and ensuring accountability.

ii. The **administrative** system, ie., the "paper work" supporting the intervention.

iii. The **financial** system, including budgeting of the intervention system.

iv. The **learning-planning** system, i.e., the system used to monitor, to report, to evaluate and to learn from interventions.

v.   The **information-communication** system that ensures that all staff and other organisations have the information they need to function properly.

vi. The **fund-raising** or resource securing system; i.e., the way that resources are raised, and the negotiation of conditions or expectations associated with these resources.

vii. The **decision-making** system, i.e., the structured involvement of designated people in making choices.

viii. The **personnel system**, involving recruitment, employment, induction, motivation, development of necessary skills, knowledge, attitudes and values (SKAV).

ix. The **environmental sensing or scanning system**; i.e., the mechanisms ensuring that the organisation stays in tune with its environment, responding where it has to, modifying the environment when it has the opportunity to do so.

x. The **accountability** system, i.e., the way that staff are held accountable for what they do, and what the organisation achieves with its resources.

To these systems can be added more abstract factors of organisational **culture, leadership and management style** and so on.

An organisation's **structure**, i.e., the way that work is split up and recombined with associated authority and responsibility, provides the basis for how systems inter-relate, and is a strong factor in determining effectiveness. Organisation development may involve changing both structure and systems.

The figure overleaf brings together a number of issues in the institutional and organisational development of service NGOs discussed earlier and is referred to in the text which follows.

The systems view makes clear, for example, that training and human resource development cannot simply be equated with institutional or organisational development. Training can only tackle a limited number of systems in only one sort of way – through the knowledge and skills of individuals or groups.

The skill of organisational development specialists lies in helping organisations to identify correctly what combination of system, structure, style or environmental factor is limiting performance, and to select the right mix of tools, methods and strategies to bring about the required changes.

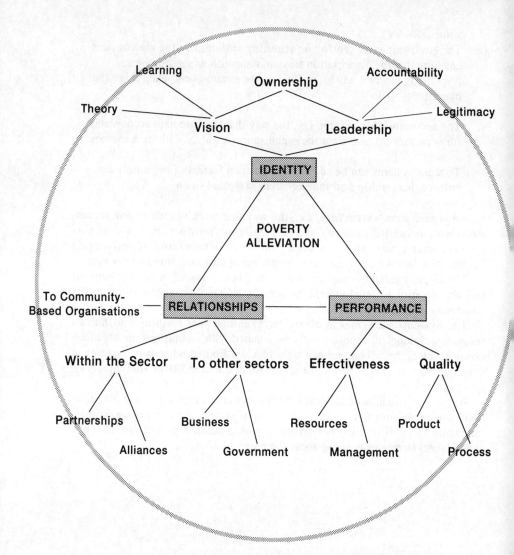

Fig. 1.   Factors in organisation development of service NGOs

6
Organisational Development Needs
of African NGOs

6.1 The Needs of African Service NGOs

Section 2.3.2 highlighted some of the reasons why African service NGOs have organisational problems. They can be briefly summarized as:

1. rapid, *ad hoc* growth; most NGOs have not been designed they just 'happen'.

2. attraction of (technical) staff who do not already have a voluntary ethos, so they have to learn one.

3. rates of expansion – due to official aid – that do not allow a natural growth of a leadership cadre within the NGO community.
    (see Appendix II).

4. being forced into development roles or methods that may not suit them, or for which staff are poorly equipped.

5. mirroring structures of Northern partners that may not be a suitable expression of their own identity, or optimal for what they want to do.

6. being unable to engage with the official aid system from a collective position based on a common understanding.

The weaknesses resulting from these problems have, in the past, been viewed in terms of staff training needs, so in the eighties numerous studies of the training needs of African NGOs were commissioned by official aid agencies and by some NGOs themselves. There is only one study known to us that has looked more broadly at issues of institutional development of African service NGOs, carried out as part of the planning for what is now to be known as MWENGO – a Centre for NGO Study and Development for NGOs of Eastern and Southern Africa to be based in Harare. This exercise brought out two distinctive strands in the self-development needs of African NGOs in the region. These could be called the long term, strategic needs and the immediate, functional needs.

6.1.1 Strategic needs

Strategic needs relate most strongly to the issues of identity and relationships shown in figure 1. African NGOs need to define more clearly their own role and perspective on development in their countries and regions rather than simply taking on the tasks allocated to them by official aid and by the state. Satisfying these needs can seldom be achieved simply by *ad hoc* training. What is required is a strategic, long term plan for organisational direction and structural change, together with an investment in the organisation's staff at all levels. Leadership development will be particularly critical. As African NGOs become more self-assured and effective, issues of organisational structure and (re)design will probably become a common source of difficulty in organisational development for them, as will their relations with the state and donors.

Support for the institutional development of NGO umbrella or collaborative bodies, platforms and networks also fulfils a strategic need, as it enhances the ability of the NGO community to engage other actors with a more coherent and stronger voice.

Strategic needs will usually contain institutional aspects, i.e. wider relations, legal framework, national development policies and social positioning.

6.1.2 Functional needs

The East Africa survey confirmed that while many NGOs have strategic needs, they are often overridden or put on the back burner because the real world of project-based financing demands better performance today. In other words, service NGOs are under constant pressure to improve their operations. Functional needs are typically those of participatory planning and project design, proposal writing, budgeting, reporting, coordinating, cost-effectiveness, quality, dealing with visitors, administration and the like.

Training staff to fulfil their roles more competently is a common path used to improve performance. However, it is almost certain that training will only fully contribute to effectiveness if it is part and parcel of an organisational development plan or programme.

Functional needs are more likely to be limited to the realm of organisational development: they do not necessarily involve the institutional level.

6.2 The Needs of Community-based Organisations

The task of service NGOs is to facilitate the institutional and organisational development of people's organisations while improving their material circumstances. The role of field staff as change agents is central to success in reaching this goal. The rest of a service NGO is there to ensure that change agents can function effectively – for they are the cutting edge of development and must not become a marginalised periphery.

Activities with local communities should contain at least three elements of institutional development: a sectoral, a managerial and an empowerment process. While we discuss these separately, they inter-relate, being combined within the intervention methods and processes chosen by the service NGO.

6.2.1 Sectoral needs

Success in poverty alleviation involves concrete improvements in people's lives, sometimes called sustainable benefits. However, the process of achieving such outcomes determines if they will be sustainable or not and is critically dependent on the right type of participation. Peter Oakley (1991) identifies the characteristics of "authentic" participation required by development in agriculture, natural resource conservation, forestry, health, irrigation and water supply. Appropriate participation depends on the way local institutions work, an important area for organisational development.

Different types of technical interventions, frequently referred to as development sectors, call for different skills and divisions of labour within community organisations. The organisational development needs of community-based organisations for a variety of sectoral interventions have been comprehensively and well documented by Norman Uphoff (1986). These include credit, agriculture, water supply, health care, natural resource management, non-agricultural enterprise, and local infrastructure development. His book is necessary reading for the managers of African, and European NGOs.

6.2.2 Organisation and management

Different types of development demand different local organisational structures and associated responsibilities. For example, the frequently male-dominated farmers' associations on irrigation schemes control an individual's access to water. Their organisational objectives and structure would not be the same as those of a primary health care committee comprising men and women who would be responsible for financing the drug supply and managing the preventive health work of a member of the community. Again, Uphoff's book provides detailed information on organisation demands of different types of intervention. The organisational development approach chosen must reflect these distinctions.

The managerial needs of people's institutions are a less well understood and documented area of organisational development. Two significant approaches to improving community management have been used to date. First, is the leadership development approach that seeks to build up group cohesion, equitable division of tasks and benefits, accountability and motivation. This approach stresses the need to assist communities to identify problems and, after setting priorities, to decide how to solve them.

The second approach emphasises project management, focusing on the control, and accounting for, of externally provided resources. Primary concerns are planning, financial control, accounting, accountability, inputs, outputs, etc..

6.2.3 Empowerment

This aspect of local institutional development focuses on the creation of awareness, based on socio-economic analysis. Typically, it has a Freireian perspective on social change, and stresses solidarity and mutuality of responsibilities within local communities and groups, as well as the structural nature of poverty and powerlessness.

Leadership training or development education are terms commonly used to describe this sort of activity, in situations where governing regimes are suspicious of emancipation as a legitimate goal of NGO action.

6.2.4 Gender issues

A number of gender issues are associated with the organisational development of community-based organisations. The most critical, in gender mixed groups, is to overcome the historical disadvantages of women in terms of education, social position and work load. Organisational development strategies need to recognise and build-in compensation for this imbalance in ways that are not divisive, for example by not relying on literacy.

There are seasonal differences between the work demands of men and women in rural areas. This means that women may not be as able to engage in and benefit from organisational development activities in the same way and to the same degree as men. The timing of organisational development must take this imbalance into account.

In women's groups, especially those initiated by the state or politicians and relying on external finance, a common organisational development issue is that not all women share the same problem to the same extent. For example, a womens' tree nursery where seedlings are meant to produce trees for farms may take too long to yield a return on the time invested by women who may need additional income in the short term. Their energies could be better served by another activity, such as retail trading.

Often the formation of groups just because of gender hides the diversity of interest and needs of members, leading to very uneven motivation and limited cohesion. Organisational development needs to accommodate diversity of priorities of group members. It cannot be assumed that because a group is homogenous in terms of gender that it is coherent or unified in its members' goals.

7
What Resources are Available for NGO Institutional Development in Africa?

Present understanding of development processes confirms that the important roles of service NGO are (a) to assist in the institutional development of community-based organisations and (b) to influence the policy arena in the North and the South to the advantage of the poor and the powerless. In other words, service or intermediary NGOs must be skilled both at enabling and supporting the strategic and functional needs of CBOs in relation to the three components detailed in 5.2 above, and at clarifying and articulating the case of the poor, i.e. at advocacy. This section of the study, therefore, reviews the resources available, or emerging, in Africa that will better equip service or intermediary NGOs to fulfil these functions cost-effectively.

7.1 A Changing Landscape

Since the mid eighties, there has been a rapid increase in availability of institutional development resources being offered to NGOs on the continent. This growth is still being fuelled by the number of new financiers, especially by bi-lateral and multi-lateral donors, that are working with NGOs. In addition, traditional donors to African NGOs are giving greater priority to institutional development as a legitimate need, although it is not easy to link institutional development to the material projects and outcomes expected by the general public.

Mapping this landscape is difficult because of the speed of change, the diversity of agencies involved in creating a greater supply of services and the lack of transparency about what is going on. A common feature throughout the continent is that the growth in supply is responsive, *adhoc* or chaotic, unevenly distributed between countries, often opportunistic in nature and not equally accessible to the (smaller) African NGOs that need it most.

Substantial growth in funding for NGO institutional development is giving rise to concerns about the quality and relevance of what is on offer. Unfortunately, there is **little in the way of substantive impact evaluations to demonstrate the suitability and effectiveness of what is provided.** In fact, the evaluation of institutional development for non-profit developmental organisations is a virtually barren field in terms of indicators and methods. Progress and quality control in institutional development of NGOs urgently requires practical measures of both institutional and organisational change. For the moment, therefore, assessments of supply and suppliers must rely on their track record and origins.

What follows is an analysis of this changing landscape as viewed by the authors of this study. It is not based on an up-to-date systematic field survey: it is inevitably impressionistic, and it will suffer from patchiness in terms of continental coverage. The analysis includes new initiatives known to the authors. One useful but dated reference source that can be consulted is the NOVIB directory authored by Cees van Dam in 1986. Other sources are national NGO directories that are slowly emerging, and the quarterly newsletter, *NGO Management*, produced by the International Council of Voluntary Agencies (ICVA) in collaboration with Southern NGOs.

7.2 Profile of Suppliers

The suppliers of institutional development services to NGOs can be placed in four major groupings: specialist NGOs, NGO development centres, governmental institutes and consultancy firms. We will detail each of these in relation to their demonstrated or likely ability to provide services to NGOs in the areas of **(i)** institutional development, **(ii)** organisational development of the NGO itself, including the forming of change agents and **(iii)** the self-development of community-based organisations.

7.2.1 Specialist NGOs

The demand for institutional development services has led to the growth in supply of specialist NGOs to provide them. National examples in East and Southern Africa are Voluntary Agencies Development Assistance (VADA) in Kenya; the Uganda Rural development and Training Programme (URDT) and the Community Development Resource Association (CDRA) in South Africa. VADA concentrates on organisational development for NGOs, and relies mostly on training courses; URDT originally specialised in change-agent training and has expanded to include information transfer; and, CDRA uses an intensive consultancy approach to institutional and organisational development of service NGOs.

In West Africa NGOs providing organisation development services include: CESAO in Burkina Faso; the INADES Formation headquartered in the Cote d'Ivoire; IRED with offices in Niger and other countries; PREFED and IWACU in Rwanda; DARD in Zaire; ATICA in Cameroon; FONGS in Senegal; SALID in Cameroon; the Centre for Community Studies, Action and Development in Ghana (CCSAD); and, ITA/PAID that operates in countries throughout the continent. Most of these agencies provide training in development project planning and management for both service NGOs and community-based organisations. CCSAD, for example, tackles institutional development issues, including sector analysis and NGO-state relations through organised studies and workshops. INADES is an acknowledged specialist in distance education in agriculture and development management.

26

The approach and skills of most specialist NGOs were initially oriented to training of NGO staff and community members. Only CDRA began with an institutional development approach and does not rely on, nor stress, training as an instrument for change. However, as a result of experiencing the limits of training for improving organisational performance, many specialist NGOs have now moved to provide *appui* or long term organisational consultancy services. A similar trend is noticeable in the *accompaniment* approach being adopted by South American providers of organisational development services to NGOs.

As the staff of specialist NGOs have, more often than not, learnt on the job, they cannot always be relied upon to have formal qualifications for what they do. It is, therefore, important to learn of the background of individual staff members and to assess their understanding of the NGO world in order to ensure that we are not in a position of the blind leading the blind. In our view, specialist NGOs tend to provide the most appropriate services, but even they find difficulty in engaging in organisation development as opposed to training and information services, because there are many difficulties in raising funding for a more extensive involvement with their clients.

Assuming that staff have origins and experience within the voluntary sector, we should expect the strength of competent specialist NGOs to lie in two areas. First, in the organisational development of service NGOs as organisations, and second in the improvement of change agent skills and intervention methods that support the organisational development of local people's organisations. Staff of specialist NGOs whose experience derives from working with community-based organisations are probably not likely to be particularly competent at addressing issues of institutional development as defined in this study. And, although there are exceptions such as PREFED, staff background and expertise would tend to orient them towards the functional rather than the strategic needs of NGOs.

This being said, pressures coming from the UN system to strengthen NGOs and their relations with governments are drawing these specialist agencies into the area of institutional development. And this is where specialist NGOs are meeting competition from governmental institutes.

7.2.2 NGO Development Centres

There is a recognised gap in the market for support services that operate at the strategic and institutional levels of African NGO need. Africa lacks organisations similar to DESCO in Peru and PRIA in India. A number of initiatives are, therefore, being taken to redress this situation. We have already mentioned the new NGO Study and Leadership Centre to be established in Harare to serve the needs of East and Southern Africa. The emphasis of this centre is on leadership forming, reflection on development issues and research from an NGO perspective. Another initiative, but with a global orientation, is soon to commence operation. The *El Taller* Centre is to be located in Tunisia, and will support NGO institutional development within and between regions of the South as well as North-South. One of its ideas is to provide a mobile squad of experts from within the world-wide NGO community who will be available to provide necessary support.

A further example of a new NGO Centre concentrating on institutional issues associated with conflict resolution and human rights is to be found in Ethiopia. The Centre for Dialogue on Humanitarian, Peace and Development is to be established in Addis Ababa. It will provide a specialist resource for NGOs operating in conflict areas.

Appendix III provides an overview of the proposed activities of these new Centres.

The embryonic nature of these new initiatives means that little can be said about their performance. We can, therefore, only assess their potential, based on the care that has gone into their creation and the credibility and expertise of the individuals involved. To date, the processes employed to define the function and ownership of these centres has ensured full involvement of the NGO community. The people promoting the idea and realisation for these centres all have an extensive history within the NGO community. The prospect of them providing qualitatively sound and relevant services appears to be high.

The comparative advantage of these centres lies at the institutional, rather than the organisational, level, with a corresponding bias towards strategic issues. This does not mean that they cannot or should not provide functional services. Indeed, the multi-national nature of their clients allows them to capitalize on South-South learning and exchange. We cannot, however, expect them to work cost-effectively with change-agents to improve the local institutional development of CBOs.

7.2.3 Governmental institutes

Market forces are causing a number of governmental training institutes in Africa to reorient their services towards NGOs. The Pan African Institutes of Development in West, Central and Southern Africa, although created as an NGO in 1964, has built up an expertise oriented towards the needs of the public sector. Since the mid eighties PAID, as with other government oriented institutes, such as the Mananga Training Centre in Swaziland and the East and Southern Africa Management Training Institute (ESAMI) in Tanzania, have a priority to engage more with NGOs (Stanneveld, *et al*, 1991). These bodies are modifying existing courses to include an NGO component or orientation, and running workshops, carrying out studies and participating in evaluations. In this process they are exposing NGOs to a more administratively-based approach to development which may satisfy, in a limited way, the functional level of organisational development needs. Their historical role of dealing with governments should also enable them to offer some assistance in the institutional development of the NGO sector, but not from the perspective of the sector itself.

In relation to NGOs, the problems of government training institutes are to do with relevance and ethos. The involvement of these institutes with NGOs is a sensible response to market forces and the shifts in donor priorities and funding on the continent. This does not mean that they have any particular competence or insight with regard to the specific management and organisational needs of the NGO community. Their heavy bias towards courses and training of government staff does not lead us to believe that they can really undertake or support organisational development of NGOs as a process. Their detachment from the grassroots makes it highly unlikely that they will be a potential path for improving the ability of service NGOs to facilitate the institutional development of local communities and people's organisations.

Further, we do not expect that these institutes will be able to handle the informal nature of NGO development work, i.e. the comparative advantage of NGOs operating with traditionally organised community groups alongside the prescribed systems of development administration imposed by the state.

We cannot foresee that these institutes will ever carry a non-governmental ethos or culture, nor understand the more complex management and organisational needs of NGOs, which are far more environmentally dependent than are nation states. The common approach of these institutes is to treat non-governmental organisations in "user" terms, as instruments of state development, rather than as autonomous actors with their own points of view. Political aspects of the NGO presence and work are not likely to be stressed or even acknowledged.

7.2.4 Consultancy firms

The growing contribution of overseas aid to government budgets, emphasis on business enterprise and promotion of local – as opposed to foreign – consultants is having two major effects on the services available to NGOs. First, it is stimulating the creation of African consultancy firms and freelance individuals specializing in development issues. Some are established and staffed by people with an NGO back ground, such as MATRIX in Kenya and SIMACON in Zimbabwe. Others are initiated by academics, former bureaucrats and entrepreneurs attracted by market growth in the sector.

Second, established consultancy firms, and especially accountancy organisations, are expanding their portfolios to include non-governmental organisations. Price Waterhouse, Ernst and Whinney are but two accountancy firms with this explicit strategy. Official donors have confidence in the reputation of such organisations and are commissioning them to undertake NGO financial audits that more often than not identify organisational problems.

Overall, the strength and usefulness of these firms depends on the individuals involved. Their background dictates their areas of competence. Scheduled training requires a level of investment that such firms are unlikely to make. They are more market oriented and responsive, offering contract-based, custom made, long term organisational development work with NGOs, and can be competent in providing such a service if they have the right experience.

Accountancy firms will have a natural bias towards NGO functional needs and an economic view of NGO work. Again, they are less likely to pre-invest in designing NGO training programmes, than to work on a contract basis. Their developmental insights will probably be minimal. They do not have the background or culture necessary to assist NGOs in the realm of institutional development.

7.2.5 Summary
The following table summarizes what we believe to be the potential contribution of the four types of service provider noted above to satisfying the needs of African NGOs.

Type of supplier	NGO Institutional Development	NGO Organisational Development	Development of CBOs
Specialist NGOs	Unlikely to be a major strength	Very suitable for functional issues with a potential for strategic issues as well	Highly relevant and suited
NGO Development Centres	A major strength	Secondary strength	Unlikely to be suitable or cost-effective
Government Institutes	Selectively useful	Suited for functional training only	Probably unsuitable
Consultancy Firms: 1. Dedicated firms. 2. Accountancy firms.	Selectively useful Unsuitable	Good for true OD Functionally useful	Uncertain, depends on the individuals Unsuitable

Table 1. Probable comparative advantage of suppliers in relation to NGO needs

7.2.6 Conclusions
i. There are too few specialist agencies or individuals in Africa able to adopt a truly organisational development approach of working with NGOs over the extended period that is proven to be necessary. This lack is partly because donors have preferred to support training rather than the

necessary longer-term involvement of a consultant. Training offers a clearer, defined package of what is being supported, and is thought to be less costly. This point is debateable if the costs of a consultant are spread over all the staff he or she is involved with. More importantly, training of individuals seldom improves the organisation's overall performance, as it ignores critical issues of structure, decision-making, personalities and management styles.

ii.   The overall demand for NGO institutional and organisational development services is not matched by a sufficient and appropriate African supply. There is a greater availability of functional training and organisational development services than there is of strategic and institutional development services.

iii. The quality of the existing and planned supply of services is strongly dependent on the individuals involved. Their track record is the best guide to the relevance and value of what is offered.

iv.   The growth in local services to African NGOs is a demand-based, but supply-(funding)-oriented free for all.

v.   There is an acute shortage of competent African (and non-African) specialists in NGO institutional and organisational development.

vi.   There are few, if any, agreed and suitable standards by which (the change) in NGO organisational functioning can be measured or assessed. They are urgently needed to assess performance, quality of services and learning.

8
Issues for European NGOs

The analyses contained in previous sections point to a number of issues that should concern European NGOs wishing to engage in organisational development in Africa. They can be grouped under the heading of policy coherence and funding strategies. In reviewing the issues we will provide recommendations for future discussion.

8.1 Policy Coherence

8.1.1 Profiles of national and regional supply
There is little coherence in the availability of institutional development services for NGOs within and between African countries. National NGO umbrella bodies, when funded to do so, attempt to identify NGO training needs, but they seldom survey or assess supply. Lack of coherence is due, in part, to lack of information, but is also due to the fact that no one body is taking the lead in providing it. By default, the most active funders in the field – such as USAID or UNDP – steer the market and define the product. European NGOs can at least avoid making the situation worse, and can improve things, if they collaborate in forming their strategies towards ID funding in each African country.

A critical area for ensuring policy coherence is between the institutional and organisational levels described above.

Policy coherence is also needed, country by country and regionally, in terms of how supply is to be increased and qualitatively improved. Table 1 above can be used as a framework for determining the information needed to reach initial policy conclusions.

The nature of the demand for institutional development services to NGOs is much clearer than what is happening in terms of the supply. Given all of the foregoing we would:

recommend   that European NGOs undertake (or commission) a supply assessment in each African country. The output would be a profile of the services available to NGOs with critical observations on capabilities and quality. Dividing up the work between agencies, each taking the lead for one or more countries depending on existing experience, would be cost effective. This study already provides categories for such a survey at the institutional and organisational level, and by type of supplier. Gaps, strengths and weaknesses are obvious entry points for policy formulation in relation to country-specific strategies of European NGOs.

While this is being done, European NGOs can already use the framework provided by this study and their existing country strategies to decide where they wish to prioritise their funding. For example, it can be used in deciding when to assist in the creation of new institutions, when to strengthen existing ones, when (not) to support training but finance longer-term consultancy for true organisational development, etc.

8.1.2 Harmony between institutional and organisational development

The relations between organisational and institutional development of NGOs are complex and our understanding is sketchy. What we need are more concrete examples of how each could and should support the other in order to identify preferred practices. We therefore:

recommend   that European NGOs document a number of case studies that illustrate and analyse the interplay between the institutional and organisational development of NGOs and of their interventions in support of the institutional development of CBOs. Such an exercise should bring out what changes in policy environment are needed to ensure NGO effectiveness at the local and national levels. It will help us to understand the conditions under which the state and donors can be successfully engaged by African NGOs, and in what ways. Comparative experience from other continents probably offer helpful comparisons.

The recent impact study on the four Dutch co-financing organisations provides a number of important insights. One of these is the finding that over the long term the quality of development projects and programmes depends on the coherence between institutional and organisational development. Proven ways to link the two cost-effectively, based on existing practice, need to be identified and shared.

8.1.3 Balancing resources for supply and demand

European NGOs face demands for institutional development funding from both potential clients and suppliers of such services. Our analysis confirms that both need financing. The questions that arise are: **(a)** with limited resources, how to achieve the most cost-effective mix of supply that is coherent nationally, sub-regionally and internationally; and, **(b)** how to achieve the right proportion between supply and demand.

Funding supply has drawbacks (see 8.2 below) and, on balance, must be a second choice. But in Africa's current condition it is vital to increase the availability of appropriate services. Supporting the suppliers tends to be a long term commitment, in other words it mortgages funds, and must, therefore, be justified from a strategic point of view. Any strategy must ensure an increase in supply that satisfies the three types of need summarized in table 1. Satisfying the demand side typically involves shorter term funding to service NGOs and community-based organisations, and its outputs are more readily identified. This should be less problematic.

Given the long term investment nature of increasing supply, European NGOs will benefit from collaboration in prioritising and sharing support to the new NGO institutions being created and to those that justify strengthening. To this end we:

recommend   that European NGOs reach collaborative agreements on strategies aimed at a balanced increase in the supply of institutional development resources in and for Africa, for both the suppliers and the clients.

What we are looking for is a mutually supported strategy that balances the very necessary investment – core funding – in order to make good the lack of appropriate institutional development resources in Africa, with the funding of institutional development for local NGOs as effective clients of such suppliers (see 8.2).

8.2 Funding Demand to Control Supply

8.2.1 The need for effective client-led demand for ID services

Donors usually respond to NGO demands for services by funding a supplier. While it is the simplest, this approach has a number of short and long term disadvantages. **First**, the supplier may become more steered by, and responsive to, the funder than to the client. In the course of time, suppliers may not keep up with market changes and so become irrelevant. Suppliers provide what they think is wanted, which may be different from what the client needs. And, because the client is not paying, inappropriate services may be accepted because they are free. **Second**, if the client is not paying for services the commitment to make full use of them is diminished. **Third**, the supply side remains uncoupled from the local economy and could appear to be an extension of the donor in another guise. Dependency is an obvious danger in this situation. **Fourth**, decisions on funding projects become all too easily linked to conditions about organisational development, with the donor-funded supplier possibly perceived as an informant about the internal workings of the partner. We therefore:

recommend   that wherever possible European NGOs fund partners to hire institutional development services rather than funding suppliers.

For example, some donors are including as (almost) standard practice a sum for ID assistance in each project grant wherever this is appropriate. This sort of practice should be encouraged, together with information on what supply is available (see 8.1.1).

8.2.2 Building European NGO collaboration

How can potential problems described above be avoided? The most secure and innovative way is to finance clients (partners) to hire the services they need rather than to fund a supply. This involves some risk because partner NGOs are not always in a position to select what is most appropriate and cost-effective for them. But it is the preferred route to travel, and the country profiles recommended earlier will help all parties in such negotiations. Second, a division of labour is required between European agencies where, for example, one concentrates on supporting institutionally-oriented suppliers, another organisational development specialists, the third local institutional development services, etc. This reduces competition and builds up expertise within an agency. The drawback is a potential monopoly by one organisation in each section. An alternative method is to form collaborative pools that share requests and decide for each case who is in the best position to respond in relation to country or regional policy priorities, existing programmes of support and so on. The importance of institutional development is unlikely to diminish. And it is a generic issue of importance on all continents, not just Africa. We would therefore:

recommend   that European NGOs consider setting up an institutional development reference group to provide an ongoing resource for further development of this field.

8.3   An Institutional Development Checklist for European NGOs

No two NGOs are the same. It is, therefore, impossible to make a detailed list of things to be considered when deciding to support institutional development. What we can provide is a summary of items to be born in mind when assessing institutional development proposals or the design of programmes.

1.   Wherever possible, staff or community training must not be funded in isolation from institutional or organisational development, or at least from some demonstrated reflection on the subject by the NGO concerned. If there is no ID or OD idea, find out why and try to stimulate it.

2.   Funding clients to pay for services – with an own contribution – should take precedence over funding suppliers directly. Proposals should

provide convincing reasons when this is not possible.

3. Preference should always be given to organisational development rather than just to training.

4. Make sure the type of NGO to be assisted is clear – single gender, dual gender – informal or formal – and that the organisational development proposed takes into account gender, and the issues of sectoral suitability, appropriate management and empowerment detailed in 6.2.

5. When assistance is provided to a service supplier this must be in the context of a strategy aimed at increasing the level of self-financing from sale of services, even if it is impossible to achieve 100%.

6. Use the systems list (5.2), issues in figure 1., and the summary of organisational development needs of service and community-based NGOs (5.1), to be clear about what organisational improvements are being aimed at. Are the methods proposed consistent with these aims?

7. Be sure that the organisation to provide the services is the most appropriate to do so (table 1). If in doubt, check their track record (via country studies).

8. Be sure that the link between institutional development and organisational development is spelt out if institutional change is the goal.

9. A proposal for assisting institutional development should be assessed against the three priorities and seven approaches listed in 5.1. Does it further these aims, if not why should it be a priority?

10. Ensure that organisational development proposals include information on important aspects of the institutional environment, e.g., government policy towards NGOs, the presence and functioning of NGO collaborative associations, the actions of official aid donors, etc.

11. Do funding requests for institutional development bear a realistic relation to the organisation's core budget, rather than to total turn over? In other words, are the organisations funding development projects carrying their share of organisational development costs? If not, is it appropriate to subsidise their programmes?

12. Ensure that details are included on how the organisation will evaluate the outcomes of institutional development activities.

9
The Need for Complementarity: An Emerging Challenge for European NGOs

This study has focused on the institutional and organisational development needs of African NGOs. It has stressed that, as organisations, all NGOs are open systems substantially dependent on their environments. And, for African NGOs, the behaviour of Northern partners is a critical environmental variable. Equally, however, what is occurring in Africa and to partners has organisational consequences for European NGOs if they wish to remain effective and relevant. In other words, one's own institutional development must be seen as part and parcel of a European NGO's strategy towards this issue on the continent. While not specifically included in the terms of reference for the present study, on the basis of discussions held with NOVIB staff on the draft report the authors felt that an initial reflection on institutional development for European NGOs will contribute to the usefulness of this study.

9.1 Dealing with Turbulence

In the words of Ali Mazrui, Africa is "a Garden of Eden in Decay": a continent plagued by economic decline, peripheralised in the global market, increasingly politically unstable and facing escalating ecological degradation. These factors all increase the "turbulence" of the environment in which NGOs have to work.

But, as argued in section 3.3.2, while turbulence creates risks it also offers windows of opportunity. The ability of a European NGO to reduce risk, to recognise opportunity and to respond properly to need will depend on its own organisation. While no two NGOs are the same, some institutional rules of thumb can be offered, indicating what is likely to be important for effective organisational functioning towards Africa. Two factors are essential – information and organisational flexibility.

In rapidly changing situations, such as in South Africa, accurate information on what is happening is vital to decision-making. Ensuring that one's ear is well to the ground becomes increasingly important. Some form of trusted local presence is, in our view, a necessity to ensure that the right sort of "NGO perspective" information is gathered on an ongoing basis.

Good information is only of use if an organisation is able (a) to process it and (b) to translate it into timely action. Processing depends on staff, their number and competence. Responsiveness depends on the flexibility built into the system for dealing with the unexpected. For funders such as NOVIB, this would mean an unallocated pot of money quickly available to support innovation and to grasp opportunities. A too carefully constructed forward financial plan allocating all funds for a year, while administratively attractive, becomes self-limiting and dysfunctional for dealing with situations which are inherently unstable. An additional component in responsiveness is the level in the organisation at which the authority to fund is located. Selecting the best level has to do with the ever-present tension between trust and control within an organisation. Given the nature of NGOs and the values we aspire to, we must move towards trust, with procedures that provide sufficient checks and balances without being a straight-jacket. Experience of NGOs confirms that, in the last analysis, it is staff acculturation with the values of the organisation that give the greatest security of decisions being consistent with agreed priorities and goals: procedures alone are no real solution.

9.2 From Networks to Strategic Alliances

The 1980s have seen a shift in NGO development strategies towards influencing public policies. This move stems from the realisation that the benefits of micro-projects can be undermined or negated by state policies that work against the poor. Not all NGOs are, or need to be, equipped to address macro and policy issues, because this often is simply duplication and allows existing power structures to exploit any differences that exist between NGOs' positions, no matter how small these may be. The NGO-World Bank Liaison Committee is a case in point.

One way of providing macro-micro and issue-based linkages between NGOs has been through networks. Unfortunately, this term has become so misused as to be virtually meaningless. Institutionally, the characteristic of a network is that during their interaction all members retain their autonomy in decision-making. (As distinct from coordination or collaboration). This "take it or leave it" situation is suitable if information exchange is the primary purpose of membership.

However, in our view, the nature of development as it is now understood, requires concerted and commonly directed efforts between similar and dissimilar actors. For example, this study argues that cost-effective institutional development for NGOs in Africa requires a mutually agreed set of activities and divisions of labour between European NGOs. In addition, the coupling of micro and macro action and engaging different development actors may be helped by negotiated links to policy institutes, specialist centres and think tanks. One organisation cannot realistically do everything that needs to be done on its own. In other words, in institutional terms, there is an urgent need to create structured links between organisations around agreed strategic goals. We should be seeking strategic alliances between like-minded organisations who can bring together their particular institutional comparative advantages to achieve commonly agreed goals. Eurostep offers one route for doing this between NGOs, as do other NGO collaborative bodies at the European level, such as APRODEV and CIDSE. However, a number of recommendations in this study, for example 8.2.2, propose collaboration between European NGOs that must go beyond simple networking if they are to be effective.

Alliances are also an important instrument for dealing with turbulence that originates from many sources as it does in sub-Saharan Africa. No one organisation can be expected to tackle cost-effectively every source of instability that negatively impacts on the poor or marginalized people. Cooperation of a different nature from networking is called for.

The decision to join in strategic alliances is often a matter of organisational policy as it entails foregoing some "sovereignty" in return for greater impact. Alliances can also influence an organisation's public image. Sub-Saharan Africa is likely to remain a major focus for the development efforts of European NGOs. This justifies an internal debate on what strategic alliances can be forged from existing networks, and what degree of autonomy of action can be relinquished in return for better performance, impact and quality.

9.3 Relief and Development: Some Institutional Concerns

As this report was being written, Zimbabwe imposed a state of emergency: not, this time, to counter a threat from South Africa, but to enable the government to deal better with the worst drought in living memory. In the Horn of Africa, the number of internal refugees continues to rise due to continued conflict – in Southern Ethiopia, Southern Sudan and in Somalia. The demand on Europe to respond to Africa's human disasters will remain, requiring emergency aid and famine relief.

Sustainable participatory development and emergency assistance pose very different institutional demands on NGOs. They are not easy organisational bedfellows and reconciling them within one organisation is complicated and difficult. If it is not done properly an NGO can end up doing neither very effectively. How can this organisational problem be tackled?

In the late eighties, a major study was carried-out on the Sahelian experience of NGOs in merging relief and development (Anderson and Woodward, 1989). This reasonably useful book, concludes that development criteria must also and always be applied to disaster responses; specifically by analysing a community's capacity and vulnerability. This conclusion suggests that the institutional development ideas and criteria described in this study are also of use in relief situations. The questions arising are: how to link what may be separate departments in European NGOs, and how to apply developmental criteria to emergency responses.

9.4 Focusing on CBOs

Section 3.2.2 refers to increasing evidence that CBOs with traditional roots are more effective in realising sustainable development. The problem for European NGOs is that many of these organisations are informal and "invisible", making them difficult to identify and to negotiate with. Moreover, these organisations are often not "democratic" in the Western sense, nor are they gender neutral or gender balanced. This type of CBO challenges us to rethink our criteria for assistance and the instruments used for its delivery. Institutionally, we are also challenged to devise appropriate methods of organisational strengthening that do not rely, for example, on literacy, or are simply subject to modern indicators of change. Engaging with traditional CBOs is probably the most difficult but potentially important institutional development issue facing European NGOs in their African work. Thinking through how to work with traditional CBOs would be worth a detailed study of its own.

9.5 A Way Ahead

While institutional development may be a poorly defined, confusing and misused term, the issues it seeks to address – the effectiveness of organisations, and their impact on social structures and values – is real and particularly relevant to positive, sustained change in Africa. Supporting institutional development of partners will call upon new approaches, time scales, criteria and relationships for European NGOs. In this sense, institutional development is not simply a new type of project to be done "out there" but is a shift in development thinking that has consequences for European NGOs themselves, and not just for their Africa departments.

The time is ripe for an institutional development debate within and between European NGOs, to ensure that the NGO community moves ahead in a way that strengthens the sector within Europe; paralleling the advances being made by states and enterprise. How can such a debate be initiated?

APPENDIX I

References for the Managment and Institutional Development of NGOs

Note: the higher the number of asterisks the more useful the publication.

Anderson M. and Woodrow, P., 1989, *Rising from the Ashes: Development Strategies in Times of Disaster*, Westview, Boulder. ***

Balogun, J., 1990, "Enhancing the Managerial Capacity of Indigeonous NGOs in Africa", paper presented at the 12th African Association for Public Administration and Management Workshop on the Theme: Mobilizing the Informal Sector and NGOs for Recovery and Development, Abuja, Nigeria, December 3–7.

Billis, D., 1989, "A Theory of the Voluntary Sector: Implications for Policy and Practice", Working Paper, No. 5., Centre for Voluntary Organisation, London School of Economics, London, April. *

Billis, D., 1991, "Reflections on the ABC of Profit and NonProfit Organizations: Benefits and Hazards in the Exchange of Ideas", paper prepared for the Case Western Conference on NonProfit Management, Centre for the Study of Voluntary Organisations, London School of Economics, London, mimeo.

Blase, M., 1973, Institution Building: A Source Book, USAID, Sage, Beverely Hills.

Booy, D., 1989, Institutional Development: A Guide for Development Practioners, University of Guelph, Guelph, Ontario. **

Brett, E.A., 1991, "Competence and Accountability in the Voluntary Sector: Organisation Theory, Adjustment Policy and Institutional Reform", Institute of Development Studies, University of Sussex, mimeo.

Brinkerhoff, D, B. and Klauss, R., 1985, "Managerial roles for social development management", Public Administration and Development, Vol. 5, No. 2, April-June, pp 145–156. **

Brown, D., 1991, "Systems Approaches to NGO Management: Establishing Decision-Making Models for Project-Level M & E", Agricultural Extension and Rural Development Department, University of Reading, Reading, mimeo

Brown, L. D., and Covey, G.C., 1987, "Organizing and Managing Private Development Agencies: A Comparative Analysis", ISPS Working Paper No. 2129 and PONPO Working Paper No. 129, Yale University, Institution for Social and Policy Studies, Institute of Development Research, Boston, July. ***

Brown, L.D. and Covey, J.G., 1987, "Development Organizations and Organization Development: Towards an Expanded Paradigm for Organization Development",

Research in Organizational Change and Development, Vol. 1., pp. 59–87, A1 Press.

Brown, L., 1988, "Private Voluntary Organisations and Development Partnerships", reprinted from, Khandwalla, P., (Ed.) *Social Development: A New Role for the Organisational Sciences*, pp. 71–88, Sage, Newbury Park.

Brown, L.D. and Covey, J.G., 1989, "Organization Development in Social Change Organizations: Some Implications for Practice", in Sykes, W., Drexler, A. and Grant, J. (Eds.), 1989, *The Emerging Practice of Organizational Development*, NTL Institute for Behavioural Science, Alexandria, V.A. and San Diego, C.A., pp. 27–37. ***

Brown, L., 1990, "Bridging Organizations and Sustainable Development", Working Paper, No. 8, Institute of Development Research, Boston.

Brown, L. and Tandon. R., 1990, <u>Strengthening the Grass-Roots: Nature and Role of Support Organisations</u>, Society for Participatory Research in Asia, Society for Participatory Research in Asia, 42 Tughlakabad Institutional Area, New Dehli 110062, India. ***

Bryson, J., 1988, *Strategic Planning for Public and NonProfit Organisations: A Guide to Strengthening and Sustaining Organizational Achievement*, Jossey-Bass, London. ***

Butler, P. and Wilson, D., 1990, *Managing Voluntary and Non-Profit Organisations: Strategy and Structure*, Routledge, London. *

Campbell, P., 1987, "Management Development and Development Management by Voluntary Organisations", <u>Selected Occasional Papers 1986–1990</u>, pp. 19–46, International Council of Voluntary Agencies, Geneva, 1990. **

Campbell, P., 1987, "Management Programmes and Services for NGOs", <u>Selected Occasional Papers 1986–1990</u>, pp. 47–62, International Council of Voluntary Agencies, Geneva, 1990. ***

Campbell, P., 1989, "Institutional Development: Basic Principles and Strategies", <u>Selected Occasional Papers 1986–1990</u>, pp. 63–78, International Council of Voluntary Agencies, Geneva, 1990. ****

Campbell, P., 1989, "Relations Between Southern and Northern NGOs: Effective Partnerships for Sustainable Development", International Council for Voluntary Agencies, Geneva, mimeo, March.

Campbell, P., 1990, "Strengthening Organisations", <u>NGO Management</u>, No. 18, pp. 21–24, International Council of Voluntary Agencies, Geneva, July/September. ****

Cernea, M., 1987, "Farmer Organizations and Institution Building for Sustainable Development", <u>Reprint Series</u>, No. 414, the World Bank, Washington, D.C.

Commonwealth Secretariat, 1988, "Proceedings of A Roundtable on Strategic Issues in Development Management:Learning from Successful experiences", Livingstone, Zambia, 9–13 May, London.

Covey, J., 1988, "Organisation Development and NGOs", <u>NGO Management</u>, No. 10, pp.

19–21, International Council of Voluntary Agencies, Geneva, July/September.

Dartington, T., 1989, "Management Learning and Voluntary Organisations", Discussion Document No. 1, The Management Unit, National Council for Voluntary Organisations, London, February.

Dartington, T., 1989, "Management Competencies and Voluntary Organisations", Discussion Document No. 2, The Management Unit, National Council for Voluntary Organisations, London, December.

Dichter, T., 1987, "Development Management: Plain or Fancy? Sorting Out Some Muddles, Findings, Technoserve, Conneticutt. **

Drukker, P., 1989, "What Business Can Learn From Nonprofits", Harvard Business Review, pp. 88–93, July–August, Boston.

Drukker, P., 1990, Managing The NonProfit Organization: Principles and Practices, HarperCollins, New York. *

Drukker, P, 1990, "Lessons for Successful Nonprofit Governance", Nonprofit Management and Leadership, Vol. 1 No. 1, pp. 7–14, Jossey-Bass, San Fransisco, Fall. ***

Egland, J. and Kerbs. T. (Eds)., 1987, Third World Organizational Development: A comparison of NGO Strategies, Henry Dunant Institute, Geneva. **

Ellsworth, L., 1988, "Rural Institutional Development in West Africa: Some Grant-Making Principles, Report to the Ford Foundation West Africa Office, Senegal, mimeo, June.

Fowler, A., 1984, "Management at Grass Roots Level for Integrated Rural Development in Africa with Special Reference to Churches", Working Paper, No. 419, Institute of Development Studies, University of Nairobi, Nairobi, December.

Fowler, A., 1986, "Development Management: Essential Concepts and Principals", Selected Occasional Papers 1986–1990, pp. 5–18, International Council of Voluntary Agencies, Geneva, 1990. **

Fowler, A., 1988, "Non-Governmental Organizations in Africa: Achieving Comparative Advantage in Micro-Development", Discussion Paper, 249, University of Sussex, Institute of Development Studies, August. **

Fowler, A., 1989, "Why is Managing Social Development Different", NGO Management Newsletter, No. 12, International Council of Voluntary Agencies, Geneva, January–March, pp. 18–20. ****

Fowler, A., 1990, "Some Thoughts on Human Resource Development Strategy For Leaders and Senior Cadres of Non-Governmental Development Organisations in Africa", October, mimeo. (Revised version of an article published in NGO Management Newsletter, No. 15, International Council of Voluntary Agencies, Geneva, October–December, pp. 17–19.

Fowler, A., 1991, "Building Partnerships Between Northern and Southern Developmental NGOs: Issues for the Nineties", Development in Practice, Vol. 1, No.1., OXFAM

43

(UK), Oxford, March. ***

Fowler, A., 1991, "Institutional Development Through Organisational Interfacing: Experiences with Non-Governmental Organisations", Paper presented at a Working Conference on the Practice of Institutional Development, Euroconsult, 11–13 November, Arnhem, mimeo.

Fowler, A., 1992, "Prioritizing Institutional Development: A New Role for NGO Centres for Study and Development", Gatekeeper Series No. 35, International Institute for Environment and Development, London. **

Goldsmith, A., 1991, "Institutional Development for Agricultural Research: Concepts, Models and Methods", ISNAR Staff Notes, No. 91–115, International Service for National Agricultural Research, The Hague, September. ***

Hage, J. and Finsterbusch, K, 1987, *Organizational Change as Development Strategy: Models and Tactics for Improving Third World Organizations*, Lynne Reiner, Boulder and London. **

Handy, C., 1987, "Organisations in Search of a Theory", National Council of Voluntary Agencies, London.

Handy, C., 1988, Understanding Voluntary Organisations, *Pelican*, Harmondsworth. **

Harris, M. and Billis, D., 1985, *Organising Voluntary Agencies: A Guide Through The Literature*, Bedford Square Press, National Council of Voluntary Agencies, London.

Huntington; R., 1987, "Accelerating Institutional Development", PVO Institutional Development Evaluation Series Final Report, United States Agency for International Development, Office of Private and Voluntary Cooperation, Washington, September. **

IDR, 1990, "Promoting Voluntary Action For Development", Institute for Development Research (IDR), Boston, October, mimeo,

International Council for Voluntary Agencies, 1983, "Definitions of 'Non-Governmental Organisation', Voluntary Agency' and Related Terms", Geneva, September, mimeo.

International Council of Voluntary Agencies, 1984, "Guidelines for Improving the Quality of Projects in the Third World by Non-Governmental Organisations", Geneva, October. ***

International Council of Voluntary Agencies, 1986, "NGO Management Development and Training: Recent experience and Future Priorities", Report on an International Seminar held in Geneva; Geneva, February. ***

International Council of Voluntary Agencies, 1986, "NGO Management Development and Training: Recent experience and Future Priorities", Report on a Sub-Regional Seminar for East and Southern Africa, Geneva/Zimbabwe, April. ****

International Council of Voluntary Agencies, 1986–1990, NGO Management, Newsletter of the NGO Management Network, Nos.1 through 18, published quarterly, Geneva.

44

International Council of Voluntary Agencies, 1990, "Relations Between Southern and Northern NGOs: Policy Guidelines", revised, Geneva, March.

ICVA and ANGOC, 1989, Institutional Development of NGOs: An Annotated Bibliography, International Council for Voluntary Agencies and the Asian NGO Coalition for Agrarian Reform and Rural Development Geneva and Manila. **

Kajese, K., "African NGO Decolonization: A Critical Choice for the 1990s", in Seminar Proceedings, No. 30, pp. 5–32, Proceedings of a conference held at the Centre of African Studies, University of Edinburgh, 24 & 25 May, 1990, Centre for African Studies, Edinburgh. ***

Kanter, R.M., 1979, "The Measurement of Organizational Effectiveness, Productivity, Performance and Success: Issues and Dilemmas in Service and Non-Profit Organizations", PONPO Working Paper, No. 8, Yale University, Institution for Social and Policy Studies, Institute of Development Research, Boston.

Leach, M., 1989, "Governance and Control in Value-Based Organizations", Institute of Development Research, Boston, December, mimeo. ***

Lent, T., 1988, "5000 Years of Exeperience: Training and Organizational Development", NGO Management, No. 9, pp. 17–18, International Council of Voluntary Agencies, Geneva, April–June. **

Middleton, M., 1986, "NonProfit Management: A Report on Current Research and Areas for Development", ISPS Working Paper No. 2108 and PONPO Working Paper No. 108, Yale University, Institution for Social and Policy Studies, Institute of Development Research, Boston, February.

Oakley, P., 1991, *Projects With People: The practice of participation in rural development*, International Labour Office, Geneva. ***

Quarles van Ufford, P., Kruit. D. and Downing., 1988, *The Hidden Crisis in Development: Development Bureaucracies*, Free University Press, Amsterdam. **

Reilly, W., 1987, "Management and training for development: the Hombe thesis, Public Administration and Development, Wiley, London, vol. 7, January–March, pp 25–42.

Reenen, G-J, van and Waisfisz, B., 1988, "Final Report on Institutional Development", report prepared for the Netherlands Directorate General for Development Cooperation, IDEAS, The Hague, mimeo. **

Rooley, R. and White, J., "Management Development Needs of Voluntary Organisations", Cranfield School of Management, Cranfield, mimeo.

Smillie, I., 1987, "Northern 'Donors' and Southern 'Partners': Arguments for an NGO Consortium Approach", Paper presented at a Workshop on Strategic Issues in Development Management, organized by the Commonwealth Secretariat, held at the University of Warwick, July.

Smillie, I., 1989, "BRAC at the Turning Point: The Donor Challenge", Paper resulting from a mission to the Bangladesh Rural Advancement Committee, September and October,

1988, mimeo.

Stanneveld, A., Zevenbergen, M. and Ndonyi, A., 1991, External Evaluation of the DSO–support to: Panafrican Institute for Development (PAID), Netherlands Organisation for International Cooperation in Higher Education, The Hague.

Tendler, Judith, 1982, "Turning Private Voluntary Organisations into Development Agencies: Questions for Evaluation", Program Evaluation Discussion Series, Paper No. 12, United States Agency for International Development, Washington, D.C. **

Uphoff, N., 1986, *Local Insitutional Development: An Analytical Sourcebook with Cases*, Kumerian Press, West Hartford. *****

Uphoff, N., 1992, "Local Institutions and Participation for Sustainable Development, Gatekeeper Series, No. 31, International Institute for Environment and Development, London. *****

USAID, 1982, "Effective Institution Building: A Guide for Project Designers and Project Managers Based on Lessons Learned from the AID Portfolio", A.I.D. Program Evaluation Discussion Series, Paper No. 11, Washington, D.C., March.

——-, 1989, "Accelerating Institutional Development", PVO Institutional Development Evaluation Series, U.S. Agency for International Development, Bureau for Food, Peace and Voluntary Assistance, Washington, D.C. ***

Some Thoughts on a Human Resource Development Strategy for Potential Leaders and the Senior Cadres of Non-Governmental Development Organisations in Africa

Alan Fowler

THE PROBLEM

Staffing policies of many international non-governmental organisations (INGDOs) operating in Africa place an important emphasis on indigenization of their staff. But, while INGDOs operating on the continent have been able to achieve significant localisation of personnel at the field, junior and middle levels, the same cannot be said for their senior, leadership positions.

Basically, there is a severe lack of local people available to take on the demands and responsibilities of very senior functions in NGDOs. The reasons for this do not lie in the lack of individual Africans with the potential to lead and manage. Rather, the problem hinges on the fact that the availability of suitably qualified and experienced people coming up through the NGDO system has not kept pace with the rapid growth in number and scale of operation of NGDOs in most countries on the continent. For, in the past, NGDOs have not paid systematic attention, nor put adequate resources, into "forming" indigenous senior cadres for their own organisations and for the African voluntary sector as a whole.

This situation produces a virtual clamour of NGDOs – especially international agencies – to identify suitable candidates as head of programming, or today's deputy and tomorrow's country director. If a person is found, nine times out of ten it is through poaching from another NGDO. The shortage of African NGDO leaders and senior programming staff is a structural problem requiring a structural solution. Having been involved for some years with organisational development of NGDOs in Africa, I believe it opportune to offer some thoughts on such a solution. My purpose is consciously to stimulate activities which lead to an accelerated and systematic development of a greater number of senior African NGDO professionals. While the problem seems universal, this writing is primarily directed at international NGDOs working on the continent.

STRATEGY

In keeping with what we have learnt over the years, and reflecting on current thinking, NGDOs interested in developing staff should consider the endeavour as one of Human Resource Development (HRD) which is much more than training. HRD involves an individual in:

- acquiring appropriate values,
- developing proper attitudes,
- gaining and applying relevant skills, and,
- accumulating required knowledge.

The totality of such human development can be termed FORMING and will be referred to as such from now on. HRD emphasises that gaining the human attributes needed for a particular job and set of responsibilities is most effectively achieved by experiential processes rather than through packages or modules of formally scheduled learning, e.g., courses. Therefore, any structured attempt to promote HRD of senior staff should be built upon a strategy which views what is to be achieved as a forming process of an individual rather than simply as a training activity.

Further, when the task is one of developing staff for future leadership roles, HRD should build in possibilities for assessment of individual growth and performance as a basis for selection. This requirement would be undermined if, from the start, an individual sees him/herself as the designated heir apparent. An HRD strategy for senior cadres should therefore include opportunities for competition, making clear that future positions in the organisation depend on demonstrations of comparative merit. Thus, HRD should allow for the forming of a number of persons at once in an institutional programme.

To summarise, a strategy of HRD for (potential) NGDO leaders and senior cadres should be founded on:

– individual forming structured through real life interactions between theory and practice,
– an institutional, rather than a "one off" approach,
– comparative performance assessment.

CONTENT

The content of forming processes should obviously reflect what are already known to be the values, attitudes, skills and knowledge required for effective leadership, management and programme development of NGDOs. It is beyond the intentions of this short paper to list these, but a recent workshop at the Commonwealth Secretariat attempted to do so. Hopefully, the explanations accompanying the following items will implicitly indicate what are considered to be the necessary features of a good NGDO manager or leader. Where possible, a resource for HRD in each component is indicated. This is not intended as a definitive statement of where to go, but rather as a pointer in where to look.

1.0 Product and Process

All NGDO staff should have a detailed understanding of what the organisation is, trying to achieve, i.e., its product. This means gaining insights and experiences of the practice and theory of rural or urban development and the role of external agencies in these endeavours. Knowing how sustainable development with the poor is actually accomplished is critical to effective management. Understanding the situation of the deprived, conceptualising what are proper interactions between an NGDO and those they seek to serve – and identifying the barriers to achieving them – are absolute prerequisites for anyone who wishes to lead or manage a development agency.

Appreciating the nature of development at the (micro) household/community/village level requires a confrontation with rural reality, backed-up by some framework to understand what is going on and therefore where one might/should intervene. For example, Robert Chamber's conceptual model of the integrated causes for human deprivation – due to interrelationships between powerlessness, vulnerability, physical weakness, isolation and poverty itself – offers a basis for critical thought. Applying this model from the perspective of an outsider who wishes to intervene may clarify what an NGDO might chose to do.

What needs to be achieved must, however, be coupled to insights on how things should be done. In other words, a link must be made between products and processes. For, without the right process, benefits – if they occur – are seldom sustainable or accrue to those intend-

48

ed. An appreciation of processes by which: people's participation can really be attained; how communities can own and manage their development; how real needs can be identified; and so on, are all required by a manager or programmer. The rural development programme at the International Institute of Rural Reconstruction (IIRR) in the Philippines is one resource for introducing individuals to these issues, both experientially and theoretically.

2.0 The Context

No NGDO works in isolation. All voluntary organisations function in a context which is to a large part determined for them, not by them. Within any country, NGDOs must relate to what governments are, or are not, doing; to the development conditions and priorities officially set; to internal terms of trade; to urban-rural relations; to national structures controlling people's access resources; to local and national politics; to the information which is, or is not, available; to systems of development administration, etc.

In short, NGOs must be able to assess the context in order to set policies, devise strategies and plan their own actions – particularly where to work, who to try and work with, in which activities and by using what methods. Naturally, answering these questions will be intimately related to what has been discussed above. Thinking at the macro-level should therefore complement action at the micro-level.

One way to expose senior staff to the set of issues associated with context is through planning. Planning involves finding the right set of relations between organisational identity, product, process, resources and context. It also requires the correct selection and use of existing information together with the ability to gather and analyze new data. A number of development planning courses exist, but not all of them involve real life field situations which support theoretical work with experiential learning. A course which does, however, is one on Rural Research and Rural Policy at the Institute of Development Studies, University of Sussex.

3.0 Personal Application for Contexturalization

The third component of forming should challenge individuals to contextualize what they have experienced and learnt by applying it in their own national/organisational setting. Often, senior staff recruited into NGDOs have first or higher degrees, but little actual experience of what is happening at the grassroots when their organisation interacts with communities, government officers, other NGDOs etc. In order for potential senior staff and NGDO leaders to fully appreciate the operational reality of their own organisation a third component of forming should require them to undertake a project at the "cutting edge".

The project should seek to apply what has been gained through the exposure provided in 1. and 2. In addition the project chosen should:

a. be on a topic which contributes to improving the NGDO's effectiveness;
b. contain a clear basis for assessment of the individual's performance;
c. contribute to new learning rather than copy existing common practices.

Examples of projects could be the application of Participatory Rural Appraisal as a means of problem identification; the use of participatory research as a tool for community mobilisation; appropriate adaptation of high technology; analysis of (group) social control in relation to credit schemes; or, whatever else is relevant to the person and to the purpose of the NGO. Project definition could be guided, and assessment could be objectified, by the inclusion of knowledgeable outsiders an advisory committee to assess projects and the performance of the individual.

A necessary outcome of this period should be the personal development of the individual and their appreciation of the importance of correct interpersonal skills and appropriate attitudes towards the beneficiaries who are, in fact, the organisation's raison d'etre. The NGO is there for the people, not the other way round. The NGDO's organisational culture, values and the design of what it does should be based on the foregoing and must eventually become a part of the individual.

4.0 Understanding Organisations

4.1 Organisation and Management: Design and Functioning

An additional component of the forming process should lead an individual towards a deeper understanding of what organisations are, how they work and how they need to be managed. Too often, the important "learning on the job", or "by the seat of your pants" which most NGDO managers go through, is not supported by an opportunity for them to stand back from the organisation and look at it objectively. The end result is a personalisation of what's happening and the belief that there is no other way of doing things. A frequent consequence is a lack of adaptability in NGDO management, yet the dynamics of the environment constantly challenge organisations to learn and adapt if they want to remain effective. A manager must have the insights, repertoire of tools and self-confidence to help his/her organisation to learn from and analyze itself and then to design and guide change accordingly.

While many management training courses in the North have been tailored towards NGDOs it is only of late that attempts have been made to design learning situations which are really appropriate to the management of non-profit organisations working in the Third World. One should therefore look for management development from institutions which can demonstrate that what they do is derived from Third World experience. Quality of case studies, "hands on" experience of trainers in micro-development can be indicators of this. Selly Oak Colleges in Birmingham (UK) and the Experiment in International Living in the USA have been active in developing management training approaches relevant to NGDOs in the Third World. The quarterly Management Newsletter produced by the International Council for Voluntary Agencies (ICVA) in Geneva is a useful reference for NGDO management development resources.

By the end of this stage, the suitability of an individual for a future role as leader of the NGDO should be coming apparent. At this point a custom-made period of forming constructed within the NGDO itself would probably be appropriate for the person(s) showing the best potential. This would include visits to the headquarters, participation in international gatherings to help build-up personal networks of contacts – so getting to know the wider NGDO world from a position as member rather than observer – internal assessed task allocations and other exposures where the integration of the attributes required of a manager can be explored, challenged and tested. The custom made period should include processes which stimulate the individual to identify with and internalise the values that the organisation represents and believes in. It should also allow room for the person to decide if he or she can really behave in ways that are required of a leader or senior manager. Issues of integrity, personal style, attitude, interpersonal skills, etc., should be openly addressed.

4.2 Organisation Development (OD)

Some INGDOs (OXFAM, Catholic Relief Services, Lutheran World Relief) function as financiers to local NGDOs. Staff of this type of INGDO would therefore need to be conversant with organisation development (OD) techniques and advisers' skills, because their work would include analysis of their partner's capabilities and a consultancy-type role towards them (leaving aside the question of the power due to the funding relationship aside).

Resources in the theory and practice of OD suitable for NGDOs are difficult to find – it is a new area with few experienced practitioners offering this as a service. Hence INTRAC is now offering short courses on institutional development both of Northern NGOs and how they can best support the ID and OD needs of Southern NGOs and CBOs. As well as myself, Piers Campbell at the International Council of Voluntary agencies (ICVA) and Ian

Yates (formerly with the International Council for Social Welfare) have designed a course for training consultants in OD for NGDOs. Their method has been tested in Southern Africa and was highly valued by the participants. The Institute of Development Research in Boston, USA, have developed some expertise in this area through a number of OD studies for non-profit organisations.

An additional approach to be recommended is attachment to a consulting group – such as the MATRIX network I am part of – or individual with a proven track record. A mix of formal OD training complemented by a period of attachment – with an assessable project component – would appear at present to be the best way of exposing an individual to the realm of professional organisational development for NGDOs.

METHOD

The sequence of forming could roughly follow the outline given above, as it is founded on a sequence of interactions between theory and practice from micro to macro levels in development. The overall duration would be in the order of two years. An example might be:

Months	Activity
1 - 3	Micro level component
4 - 6	Work in normal function
7 - 9	Personal application (micro level project and reporting)
10 - 12	Macro level component (development planning)
13 - 15	Work in normal function
16 - 18	Organisation component
19 - 21	Work in normal function
22 - 24	Attachment or leadership orientation specific to the NGDO.

The actual sequence would, of course, depend on the availability and timing of the various resources selected. Assessment may lead to a discontinuation of a person in the HRD programme if they prove not to have the capacities to go further.

Costs would depend very much on the country in which the NGDO is situated and the type and location of the forming activities chosen, but would probably amount to US$20–30,000 per individual over a two year period.

INGDOs could adopt a common strategy where HRD experiences of one organisation – the effectiveness, appropriateness and quality of resources used – is shared and compared with others. This could contribute to peer group formation and promote solidarity within the NGDO community in a country. In other words, INGDOs combine forces (formally or informally) in the creation of senior African NGDO professionals as a structural contribution to the development of the voluntary development sector in Africa. Such an approach – if clearly directed at increasing the number of capable people within the NGDO sector rather than just within each individual NGDO – could also be more attractive for potential donor support.

Finally, NGOs planning an HRD strategy for senior staff must bear in mind that increasing the quality of human resources may not automatically translate into greater organisational effectiveness. For the realization of human potential can be limited or negated by inappropriate organisational design. In my view, therefore, any HRD effort is best done as part of the development of the organisation as a whole. Only then is there a reasonable certainty that the costs of HRD will translate into the benefits of enhanced organisational performance.

Revised 1990 & 1992

APPENDIX III

NGDO Self-Development Issues and the New International NGO Centres

NGDO Self-Development Issues		*El Taller*	NSDC-ESA	CDPHI
IDENTITY				
	NGDO sectoral analysis	∗ ∗	∗ ∗ ∗	∗
	Policy/theory development	∗ ∗ ∗	∗ ∗ ∗	∗ ∗ ∗
	Learning	∗	∗	∗∗
	Advocacy/lobbying	∗ ∗	∗	∗ ∗ ∗
	Leadership development	∗ ∗ ∗ ∗	∗ ∗ ∗ ∗	∗ ∗
	Accountability and ownership	∗ ∗	∗ ∗ ∗ ∗	
IMPROVE PERFORMANCE				
	NGDO management and organisation development	∗ ∗	∗ ∗	
	Professionalize staff	∗ ∗ ∗ ∗	∗ ∗	∗ ∗
	Improving interventions	∗ ∗ ∗ ∗	∗	∗
	Evaluation	∗	∗	∗ ∗ ∗
RELATIONSHIPS				
	Partnership building N-S	∗ ∗ ∗	∗ ∗	
	Alliance building S-S	∗ ∗ ∗ ∗	∗ ∗	∗ ∗
	Government-NGDO	∗ ∗	∗ ∗ ∗ ∗	∗ ∗ ∗ ∗
	Joint advocacy	∗ ∗ ∗	∗	∗ ∗ ∗

Notes:
1. The number of asterisks indicate what appears to be the relative significance of the issue for the centre concerned; the greater the number of asterisks the greater the importance.
2. A the time of writing information on the NSDC-ESA suggests that the think-tank emphasis may be chosen and is shown accordingly. This has yet to be confirmed.
3. El Taller – The NGDO Workshop – presently in Spain.
   NSDC-ESA = NGDO Study and Development Centre for eastern and southern Africa.
   CDPHI = Centre for Dialogue on Peace and Humanitarian Issues, Horn of Africa